Grandma Goes to
South Africa series

FIVE CHEETAHS

by
Linda L. Sheehan

DEDICATION

This book is dedicated to my husband Dennis- ever faithful, true, and always willing to boldly follow wherever the Lord Jesus leads us – even when it is to the *bushveld* of South Africa.

ACKNOWLEDGMENTS

Special thanks to:

Emma van Wyk, zoologist and former cheetah caretaker at a private cheetah reserve in South Africa, for sharing her love, excitement, and knowledge of cheetahs with me; Angela Onuma, my sister-in-law, who faithfully helped with proofreading; Celia Milslagle, my friend, who also gave warm encouragement and valuable suggestions for the book and stories; and Patricia Tricorache of Cheetah Conservation Fund of Namibia who proofread the book and gave me the most updated information regarding the plight of the cheetah.

Check out this website for facts in this book and more cheetah information:

Cheetah Conservation Fund. About the Cheetah. [Online] Available at http://www.cheetah.org/?nd=about. October 20, 2011.

FIVE CHEETAHS

This book contains the stories of five cheetahs. You will soon discover just how different they are. Each one lives at the cheetah game reserve. It is in the Limpopo region of the nation of South Africa.

These five cheetahs have many things in common. Every person should know about these amazing animals. Then we can each share the duty of taking care of them.

As many as 90% of cheetah cubs die before they are one year old. Too often they do not live long enough to have their own families. With one heart, we can do our part to save them and their environment from harm. You and I can help to protect these special creatures.

FRIENDLY JACO

Jaco (pronounced *YAH-ko*) was born in captivity. That means that his parents already lived in the game reserve.

Jackals attacked Jaco's mother. She was badly hurt while protecting her cubs. Animal keepers found Jaco and his injured mother. Jaco was very tiny. The driver wrapped him in a washcloth and carried him with one hand. He drove furry, little Jaco and his wounded mother to the reserve. Unfortunately, Jaco's mother died shortly after her arrival. However, Jaco found a new life here. Soon he was drinking milk from a bottle like this kitten.

The animal keepers did everything for baby Jaco. They fed him milk formula every two or three hours. A bottle with a special nipple held his warm milk. They also fed him during the night. He did not even get too hot or too cold in their care. When Jaco had a runny nose, an eye infection, or any other medical problems, his caretakers doctored him.

When Jaco was about six weeks old, his caretakers began to feed him finely chopped meat mixed with his formula. Sometimes they added eggs and powdered supplement. Jaco gobbled it up every time. Gradually, they began to feed him larger pieces of animal meat that cheetahs like to catch.

From the beginning, chubby little Jaco was a friendly African cat. He loved his caretakers. They stroked him and rubbed his ears. In return, he licked them and rubbed his head on their legs to show his affection. This cub was a very small but sociable little cheetah.

Soon Jaco grew to be a curious cub. He followed his caretakers everywhere. He tagged along as they inspected the reserve. He liked to travel with them in their truck. He was like a little shadow. Sometimes he took naps in the office and even slept on the bed!

Jaco purrs a lot. This shows he is very happy. Cheetahs are the only big cat that can purr. They often enjoy human company too. However, they are also protective. They stamp their front paws on the ground and spit or growl to frighten off would-be enemies as well.

Cheetahs are unlike other wild cats. Once tamed, they will not usually go back to being wild. However, we can never forget that cheetahs are still wild. Their natural instincts to kill and eat always exist. It does not matter how friendly they seem. It is not wise to trust all wild animals to always be friendly.

Cheetahs have always been a popular animal throughout history. In olden times, kings often chose cheetahs as their favorite animal for several reasons. They would train them to hunt impala and other wild animals. Their speed and telescopic eyesight made them great hunters. Their beauty and more gentle nature also charmed many. This is still true today.

Jaco and Mandela, another cheetah cub, grew up together at the game reserve. They bonded. That means that they developed a strong friendship. Many male cheetahs remain friends for life like Jaco and Mandela.

Jaco and Mandela

Before long, the cubs were eighteen months old. They were ready to leave their holding pens. Freedom in the wide-open spaces of the game reserve will be a great adventure. On their own, they must be careful to avoid other dangerous animals. They must also hunt by themselves. Zebras, impala, wildebeests, and even ostriches will be their targets.

Jaco and Mandela hunted together in the large reserve for two years. Even though their caretakers had hand-fed them, they naturally knew how to hunt. Their cheetah instincts remained strong. They could easily track down, chase, and kill other animals for food.

One day Jaco scrambled to escape from a lion's attack. He fell into a bush. Suddenly, his back leg was in terrible pain. He spotted a razor-sharp thorn stuck in his hip. Cheetahs will usually remove thorns by themselves, but this time Jaco could not do it. The thorn, buried deeply in his leg, hid itself.

Soon Jaco was in trouble. He had developed a dangerous infection. Caretakers took him back to the reserve shelter where they treated his wound. It is difficult to give pills to wild animals. Jaco's caretakers hid his antibiotics and medicine in his meat. He ate his medicine without even knowing. They also gave him shots and put him on a special diet. He recovered, but the infection left him with a bad limp.

This injury was dreadful for Jaco. Now he could no longer chase and kill his food. Therefore, he could not return to the free-roaming part of the reserve. Instead, caretakers brought him to a special holding area. It is a fenced-in home for animals and cheetahs much like you would find in a zoo. Here caretakers can care for him like a king.

Jaco recovers from his wounds.

Jaco is twelve years old now, but he still loves human company. He is a very loveable, friendly, and peaceful cat. Running along the fence, he follows his caretaker's truck. He purrs loudly when people arrive for a visit. Sometimes he gives his catcall so that they will scratch his ears or speak softly to him. Every now and then, he also gives his little chirping sound when people start to leave. He is telling them, "I want you to stay. Please don't go yet."

Jaco still lives happily at the cheetah game reserve today.

NELSON, THE KING CHEETAH

Nelson, his brother, and two sisters came to the reserve shelter when they were just a few days old. They were not born in a game reserve.

New cubs begin to show their spots a few days after birth.

Their mother had left her cubs to hunt for food. She alone is responsible to nurse the cubs and catch all the food for her family. Therefore, Nelson's mother was only following her natural instincts. Sadly, this time she made a natural but wrong choice. She killed a farmer's sheep.

In like manner, the farmer also made a wrong choice. He shot Nelson's mother. He wanted to protect his other animals. Even so, cheetahs are a protected species. By the laws in most countries, people are not supposed to harm them.

In some nations, there are legal penalties for shooting cheetahs. In other nations, it is legal to shoot a cheetah if it is killing livestock. Many cheetah organizations today work with farmers to learn different ways to prevent livestock losses. Losing just one goat or sheep can bring suffering for poor farmers. They may not have food for their families. Certainly, free-roaming cheetahs can be in great danger.

Cheetahs that live in the wild suffer and die like this too often. They attack farmers' animals because they are hungry. It can be very difficult for them to find food. More and more farmers put up fences to protect their cows, sheep, ostriches, and other livestock. The fences keep out the cheetahs, but the cheetahs' hunting area also becomes smaller.

So, Nelson, his brother, and two sisters were rescued and taken to the game reserve. Caretakers fed each cheetah cub milk from a bottle like a little baby kitten. It was a very busy time for the caretakers. When Nelson was a bit older, they fed him cat food instead of supplement like some of the other cubs. As usual, caretakers gradually added chopped meat to his food as he grew.

Nelson the king cheetah

Nelson is quite different from his brother and sisters. He is unique. He was born with a rare and special design in his fur. He is called a king cheetah for this reason. These unusual, vivid markings make him noticeably different from all the other cheetahs.

It certainly does not bother Nelson to be extraordinary. In fact, he rather likes it. It fits his personality. He often seems relaxed, casual, and even indifferent and uncaring. Each cheetah is one of a kind. It has an individual personality and a spot pattern that is unlike any other.

Nelson is still like normal cheetahs in most other ways. For example, he has some of the fuzzy fur on his neck that he had as a cub. He will keep some of this fluffy fur his whole life.

Animal keepers also raised Nelson as a pet, but he was not a very friendly cub. Even when he was young, he showed his teeth and stamped his foot when the keepers came. He did not like to just relax and spend time with them.

He also became a very fussy eater. He refused to eat chicken, sheep, goats or cows that the animal keepers sometimes fed cheetahs. He only liked to eat wild game like zebra, blesbok, and impala.

When Nelson was eighteen months old, it was time to release him into the larger part of the game reserve. He began to hunt for his own food at once.

Nelson could have chosen almost any small animal as his first dinner, but he had his eyes set on something big. He selected the first thing he saw, an African buffalo. It was twice as big as he was. Nelson must have been very hungry.

African buffalos travel and eat together in a big herd.

Sorry to say, Nelson soon gave up chasing the buffalo. After all, this was the first time he had a chance to practice his hunting skills. He decided to catch a smaller impala instead. A small impala is just about the right size. Nelson would not need to hunt again for a few days.

Soon Nelson met other male cheetahs in the reserve. They became friends and formed a coalition, a small group, to hunt together. This way they had more success at capturing larger prey. Together they successfully hunted and killed an African buffalo. They all ate and ate. Everyone was full. Then they lay down for a rest in the middle of the road.

Before long, a truck drove by with some visitors. They were on a game drive. People often hire a guide to drive around the game reserve. The guide shows them the different animals that live there. This is one way that a game reserve can make money. Then they use the money to support their animal projects.

Nelson and his friends enjoyed the attention. Everyone took pictures of the three full cheetahs lying in the sun.

Nelson is also part of a special project at the reserve. He wears a GPS (global position satellite) collar. The animal keepers can track Nelson everywhere he goes by using this satellite connection. This way they keep detailed records and discover important information about cheetahs.

For example, they can pinpoint Nelson's exact location and go to observe him. Using binoculars, caretakers study him without being seen. They watch to see which animals the cheetahs choose to kill and eat. They also discover how much and how often cheetahs need to eat.

Gamekeepers learn about the cheetahs' daily patterns and other habits. They watch the cheetah families grow and interact with each other. This information will help gamekeepers to make the reserve an outstanding natural environment for all the animals. They want to have everything the animals need to stay healthy.

CJ AND JOHAN
THE NAUGHTY BROTHERS

CJ and Johan are brothers. They began their stay at the game reserve with a great adventure. A helicopter brought them to the reserve when they were just a few months old.

Caretakers do not catch cubs by chasing them. They use a special tranquilizer gun. Instead of a bullet, this gun has a dart that contains medicine. This will make the cubs relax and go to sleep. They must remain peaceful during the flight so they do not hurt themselves. If they were awake, they might try to escape during the trip.

CJ and Johan woke up soon after their arrival. They were instantly very popular with the staff. Everyone soon adopted them as the favorites at the game reserve.

As they grew, they became very familiar with their caretakers. They came to know the daily schedule around the game reserve. When it was time for food to arrive, they often waited near the gate. They perked up their ears and ran toward the sound of their caretaker's approaching truck. They would give their little chirp sound or purr loudly to greet the driver.

Today, CJ and Johan are grown up. Nothing much seems to bother them. They stretch out and relax. They sit around and survey all that goes on near their holding area. The boys consider themselves to be the kings of the reserve. They prance around their pen watching and looking.

When new people come to the reserve, these two cheetahs just take a seat and stare at them. They often do not even move. They seem almost uncaring, not bothered by much. Sometimes they just sit as their caretakers bring them their food. They are lazy cats.

However, cheetahs can also be nosey animals. These two cheetahs were very nosy. One day, CJ and Johan spotted an ostrich in the neighbor's yard. They were very interested.

They kept their eyes on this strange looking animal. For days, they watched its every move. Cheetahs like to eat ostriches, and this seemed to be a great opportunity for the boys. On the other hand, the ostrich watched CJ and Johan too!

It was morning. No people were around. The boys tested the electric fence surrounding their holding pen. The electricity was turned off! This often happens in South Africa. The electricity is not always reliable. This was their lucky day. Now the ostrich became the center of their attention. Their mouths watered. Will they have a feast today?

They quietly crawled to the gate and pushed it. It opened! So they easily ran into the neighbor's yard and leaped over the fence. The ostrich ran for her life. She can run very fast, but the cheetah brothers were much faster. CJ and Johan pounced on the ostrich immediately. What a banquet they had!

Sadly, their feast and their freedom were short-lived. The farmer had heard the noise. He came running to the pen. Too bad, he was too late to rescue the ostrich. After scaring the cheetahs away, he called the caretakers at the game reserve.

Caretakers soon fixed the electric fence. They also locked the gate with a new bolt. Now the boys were home again.

Their great adventure had ended. Soon they stretched out under the tree once more. They still did not seem to be bothered by anything. Living in a cheetah game reserve was not such a bad life after all. They had full tummies and were ready for a catnap.

As members of the cat family, all cheetahs are generally lazy. They like to take many naps, especially after eating. They also like to sunbathe and, of course, play. When they are not hunting, they are usually taking it easy.

CJ and Johann have always loved to sit on high places. When they were young, they sat on anything tall. They liked mounds of dirt, an anthill, or a tree limb. Now they still like to be far above the ground. Here they can easily look around. These two brothers always like to do things together.

25

It seems the boys never learned from their mistakes. Besides getting into trouble, they both liked to torment their neighbor. He was an older cheetah. His pen was right next door.

Running up and down the fence, CJ and Johan teased him daily. They swatted their paws on the fence, hissed, and spit. The boys did not want another male in their territory. They considered themselves to be kings of the reserve.

The older cheetah was not very impressed.

CJ and Johan's caretakers drive through the game reserve to the holding pens. Daily they bring food to feed the cheetahs. One day, CJ and Johan hope to be released into this free-roaming part of the reserve. They may soon be chasing the zebras and wildebeest themselves. They would love to catch one of them for supper.

FEARLESS JULIET

Juliet was one of four cubs born to her mother. When only months old, she alone survived a lion's attack which took the rest of her family.

Days later, caretakers of the reserve found her lying on the side of the road. She was weak from hunger and near death. They brought her to the game reserve shelter for treatment. Now she lives in safer surroundings.

Early in life, Juliet knew about violence and survived more narrow escapes as she grew up. From the moment that Juliet entered her holding pen, nearby wild animals noticed her. One close encounter involved a baboon family.

Several baboons lived in the nearby mountains. Juliet's pen rested at the foot of this mountain. These baboons have a keen sense of smell, and they could smell Juliet. Baboons fear cheetahs. They all worried that eventually she might harm their troop, the baboon family. They watched Juliet very carefully every day.

One day the chief male baboon was bold and curious. He hopped over the fence into Juliet's pen. She began to growl and spit. Repeatedly, the baboon made his dog-like barking sound. His loud bark alerted the caretakers. Immediately, they ran to investigate. They discovered the huge baboon jumping and circling Juliet. Quickly, they made loud noises which frightened the baboon away. Juliet had narrowly escaped danger again.

Once, she also met a poisonous black mamba that had come into her holding area. Fortunately, the snake slithered away. Now Juliet also had experience watching for snakes. Dangerous animals also have their homes even in a game reserve. Jackals, lions, and wild dog packs are each a deadly threat to cheetahs.

This cheetah cub plays with its mother.

Juliet did not have the protection of her mother. Mother cheetahs take good care of their cubs with great devotion. They lick each other and rub their heads together. They often play together too.

Being alone is not a strange thing for Juliet. As a female, she naturally wants to be alone. She does not care to be part of a group. Juliet will live her life by herself, except when she gives birth to cubs. Then she will be the solitary family leader, provider, protector and teacher. Male cheetahs have no part in raising the cubs.

Even today Juliet still keeps to herself when the caretakers come to feed her. She turns her head as she recognizes the sound of the truck that always brings her food. She even follows the truck to her feeding place. On the other hand, she quickly runs away if someone tries to move toward her.

When her caretaker arrives to feed her, Juliet quietly comes. She crouches down and watches as the caretaker places the meat in her feeding spot. Then she quickly darts to snatch the meat. She carries it or sometimes drags it to the shade of a nearby tree or bush to eat. Like other cheetahs, she rests when she is finished.

Already Juliet has tackled many dangerous experiences single-handedly. Most of her life she has had to face frightening situations on her own. Like all events in life, they have helped her to prepare for the future.

Juliet continued to grow in size and develop her sensitivity. Soon she would be old enough to leave the holding pen. Her understanding of harmful animals will help keep her alive. In the *bush*, the free-roaming part of the reserve, she will have a new freedom to wander around the thousands of grassland acres. There it will be natural for her to defend herself. She will also have to hunt and kill her own food. Eventually, she will find a mate and have cubs of her own as well.

Today it's clear to see that Juliet has adapted well to her new freedom in the *bush*. She is a wise, brave, independent, and determined cheetah. These qualities will soon be put to the test in a new situation. Juliet will give birth to cheetah cubs.

Juliet knew the cubs would be born shortly. She made careful plans to protect her family. First, she chose a secluded place. Thorn bushes and dense thickets surrounded the new den.

Second, it was difficult to get into this new home. However, that was good because it meant that the well-protected den also made a good hiding place from enemies. Many dangerous animals nearby might try to threaten the new family.

In addition, the rainy season in South Africa was coming soon. Fires that are so common in the dry winter months were not a threat to this new home at this time of year. Therefore, Juliet was sure that she had found a safe place.

Early the next morning, the sunlight found Juliet snuggled up with five tiny balls of fur. The cubs had arrived.

Cheetah cubs are born blind, much like pet cats. After ten or twelve days, their eyes open. In addition, their dark spots and beige fur do not show up until they are a few days old. Cubs have a short, fuzzy mane of fur sticking up on their necks and shoulders.

A mother cheetah and her cubs make an affectionate family.

Like all babies, cubs are defenseless. Good mothers will fiercely protect them. They move cubs often after they are a few days or weeks old. Cheetah mothers also faithfully train the cubs to hunt as they grow. This prepares them for the time the mother cheetah will, as expected, leave them when they are between eighteen months and two years. They also teach their cubs basic social skills like who their enemies are. Juliet had learned the hard way about a cheetah's enemies. Her cubs will benefit from her experiences.

Mother cheetahs are also survivors. They must hunt for all the food for their cubs and themselves with no help. Of course, the cubs get milk from their mothers for the first three months. After that, cubs are able to begin sharing the meat mother brings to their dens.

Cheetah cubs are careful to stay out of sight when their mothers leave them to go hunting. They only come out when they hear her chirping call. Cheetah families are close-knit groups. Cubs obey and trust their mother without question. It is a matter of life and death for them. If they wander away, other animals might kill them.

There is a lot of time to relax after a good meal. In addition to napping and growing, cubs learn many things about their world as all children do.

Cubs play with each other a lot. This way they develop skills they will need to survive as adults. For example, they stalk each other. Mother cheetahs model this behavior before they attack an animal for their meal. Cubs do not want to be clumsy when they hunt for food in the future. Cheetahs only kill other animals when they are threatened or when they are hungry.

Cubs also chase, trip, and jump on one another as they learn to keep their balance. Gradually, they grow stronger and wiser. Of course, their favorite thing to do besides eat and play is to hang out with Mom.

When they are around eighteen months old, cubs will have finished their training. Mother cheetahs suddenly leave the family. Cheetah cubs usually stay together for several more months. Immediately, they begin to hunt for their own food. They still need practice to hunt well. Their mother trained them to stay alive. Eventually, the females leave the others to live by themselves. Male cheetahs are more social. They often continue to stay together in pairs or in a group.

Though her cubs were born in a game reserve and Juliet had been a wonderful mother, tragedy soon struck her family. A male lion had attacked the den. He had destroyed all the cubs while Juliet was hunting for their food. The cubs never had the chance to play, hunt, and grow as other cubs.

This male lion looks peaceful now, but lions are one of the major enemies of cheetah cubs. Lions will kill or eat the cubs, but usually will not hunt larger cheetahs.

Lions and cheetahs compete for the same prey. Lions very firmly protect their own hunting territory. Cheetahs are not welcome to hunt for the same impala, wildebeest, and zebras that the lions are hunting.

In fact, lions and some other animals are so hostile toward cheetahs that they often steal their kill. Cheetahs are not aggressive. They will give up their catch rather than risk injury in a fight for it. Then the cheetahs have nothing to eat. They must hunt again. For this reason, cheetahs eat a lot and eat it quickly after catching their prey.

Animal trainers always keep a close watch on all the animals in the game reserve. They soon noticed that Juliet did not return to the den. They knew something was wrong. Her abnormal actions alerted them. Caretakers went to investigate. As they had suspected, the cubs were all gone.

Today Juliet is expecting another litter of cubs. They should be born in about three months. The caretakers are anxiously awaiting their arrival. Soon it will be a happy time at the game reserve again. There will be a new, playful cheetah family. The feisty cubs will bounce and jump around. They will learn the ways of the *bushveld* (African grasslands) from their mother. Cheetah families can continue to exist for many years to come if you and I and other humans do what it takes to help keep them alive.

CHEETAH GAME RESERVE

Cheetahs are in danger of disappearing from the earth.

Cheetahs are, in fact, now extinct in many countries. South Africa is one of the few nations where people can still see wild cheetahs today.

A game reserve is not the answer for cheetah survival. Still, it is like a safe haven for cheetahs. This big tract of land has a special area of holding pens and buildings. It also has several thousand acres of flat land covered with grass. These acres are wide-open spaces in the country. South Africans call this the *bush*. Here cheetahs can grow and run freely.

A cheetah family finds less human danger in a game reserve. Free-roaming cheetahs on farmland can be at a greater risk. Then again, in some nations organizations are working with farmers and educating other people about cheetahs. In some countries, cheetahs live freely on farmland. Farmers are learning how to share their land with cheetahs. They even reap benefits. These practices can and have helped the cheetah population to become stable in some countries.

Generally, it is not as safe for cheetahs to live near public areas like ranches and cities. People are usually afraid of cheetahs. They have seen cheetahs attack or take livestock. People who are not "predator friendly" often just kill them. On the other hand, some will call authorities if they spot a cheetah near ranches or public property.

Game reserves, education, and understanding of the farmer's situation are each important parts of helping the cheetah survive. These animals need a protected place in which to grow. They need a place where they can safely raise a family. Well-informed people are vital to the survival of these beautiful creatures. With this combination, cheetah families have a much better chance to carry on.

WORKERS ON THE RESERVE

Quite a variety of men and women work and live at the game reserve. Animal caretakers like zoologists work here. Game rangers and reserve managers also find jobs on a game reserve. Ecologists sometimes work on game reserves too.

These caretakers have many jobs. They must know about medicine so they can give the cheetah good medical care. Caretakers also must know how to build and clean the cheetahs' homes or pens. They must repair fences too. These people also prepare the meat for cheetahs. Daily they bring this food and water to cheetahs in holding pens. They keep careful records of the other animals in the reserve, as well.

Animal caretakers also manage the larger part of the game reserve. They bring other animals to live on the reserve so the cheetahs will have food. Cheetahs living in the *bush* are different from those living in holding pens. If they live in the free-roaming part of the game reserve, they must catch food by themselves. They love to eat impala, kudu, young wildebeest, zebra, and blesbok.

Impala are among the favorite foods of cheetahs.

Animal keepers pay attention to all the game reserve animals. They make notes of their location and actions. They also study the many animal lifestyles. Studying these facts brings to light the best ways to help the animals. Making careful changes at the reserve can help the animals live a better life.

On a game reserve, it is best to have a natural balance of wildlife living together. The animals should all be happy. Caretakers determine if there are enough animals living in the reserve so that the cheetahs do not go hungry. Some caretakers may choose to remove lions, spotted hyenas, and other killers. These animals do not usually like to eat cheetahs, but often just destroy them. They do not want to share their hunting territory with cheetahs.

In winter, caretakers often put out extra food for the animals in the reserve. Lack of rain makes the game reserve dry. Grass and other plants do not grow well at this time of year. The grass that is left is not nutritious. Therefore, caretakers bring alfalfa, mineral blocks, and salt licks into the reserve. These extras help the animals stay healthy.

THE REMARKABLE CHEETAH

Cheetahs are the fastest running mammal in the world.

They can run 70 miles per hour (114 kilometers per hour) in only two to three seconds! They can reach speeds of up to 74 mph (120 km/h). One running stride can be from 23 to 26 feet (seven to eight meters) long. Cheetahs can cover 91 feet (28 meters) in one second. They are an amazing animal.

A cheetah's body is built for incredible speed. It is thin and muscular. It also has a very flexible spine. The tail helps to keep balance when cheetahs zoom after their prey. It acts like the rudder of a ship. It is about 28.5 inches long and has a tuft of white fur on the end. The wide nostrils and large lungs take in lots of air needed for this amazing speed. The cheetah needs each special feature for survival.

.   The cheetah runs so fast that it touches the ground with only one foot at a time. There are two places in the 23 to 26 foot running stride where no feet touch the ground! Now that is mind-boggling!

Male cheetahs are larger than females. The average cheetah is about four feet long. It weighs between 69-140 pounds. This small African cat is only about 30 inches tall at the shoulder. The body is very sleek and thin.

The cheetah uses the element of surprise and his startling speed typically in the morning or evening to catch his food. He stalks his prey before he runs after it. The chase lasts only about 20 seconds. Cheetahs run so fast that they tire quickly.

Watch out below!

Cheetahs usually rest after eating, but they also have fun. This is a good time to play. Cubs jump on their brothers and sisters. They run and chase each other too. They climb on rocks, tree branches, and even their mother.

Cheetahs have beautiful beige and golden yellow fur with black solid spots. These colors help hide them in the African landscape. A dark tear line runs from their eyes to their mouth. This is a very noticeable cheetah characteristic.

In the picture above, a mother and her cubs survey the African grasslands, the *bushveld*. Cheetahs get a better view from these high places. They can spot other animals that might serve as food. Then they can go down and make the kill. This is also a typical way that cheetahs pass the time.

WHO IS HELPING THE CHEETAH?

Many organizations are concerned about our disappearing animals. The Convention on International Trade in Endangered Species (CITIES) has passed special laws. These laws prevent the sale or trade of cheetahs and their skins. These laws will help keep more cheetahs alive.

Cheetahs were added to the CITIES endangered species list on July 1, 1975. This organization adds animals to this list when facts show that there are few of them alive in the world today. Though cheetah numbers are improving today, they are still Africa's most endangered cat species.

Other organizations, both private and public, make every effort to educate farmers and the public about the cheetah's situation. Learning about cheetahs and their troubles is one way we can help. When we understand the farmer's problem and the cheetah's problem, then we can find answers that will work for both. Those answers will lead to healthier cheetahs that live longer. Already, the death of cubs born in captivity has dropped from 30% to 20%. We hope to remove them from this deadly list soon. We want them to survive and multiply.

Cheetahs are smaller African cats. Sadly, their small size is part of their survival problem. Larger animals like lions and leopards kill them more easily. They also steal their food. Cheetahs usually live to be ten to twelve years old in the wild. In captivity, they can live to be fifteen or even twenty years old.

Specifically, we do not want cheetahs to disappear from the earth forever. We want them to stay alive and flourish today and in the future. That is one reason why game reserves are so widespread. Here endangered animals can grow in a somewhat safer environment. Trained animal keepers can study them. Here cubs have a better chance of surviving. The whole litter of cubs can grow up to have families of their own.

In addition, learning about cheetahs, their habits, needs, and personalities gives us an understanding of endangered animals and their problems. Knowledge gives us an appreciation for all of God's creatures, not just the endangered ones. As a zoologist, ecologist, veterinarian, or even a farmer, many young people will one day work with people and cheetahs or other animals to help solve the problems of living together. There are still solutions undiscovered. Maybe one day you will find some answers!

Cheetahs are vulnerable and valuable. These animals are powerless to make changes so that they can survive. People must make these changes. You and I must speak up to help make these changes. We can make a difference. Improvements must come or some animals will become extinct, die out. Your choices and my choices do not merely affect us. Our choices always affect other people. They can also affect other animals.

Today many of us are waking up. We now see that people have taken advantage of animals in many terrible ways in the past. We have chosen to do what always seemed best for us. Too often, we have failed to consider the animals. However, this can and must change.

Life is precious. Animals are precious. People are precious. It is possible for people and animals to all live together and prosper.

Run today

Run tomorrow

Run, Cheetah, run!

The cheetah is no longer alone in his fight for survival.

www.ingramcontent.com/pod-product-compliance
Lightning Source LLC
Chambersburg PA
CBHW041506280526
45792CB00004B/1145